Collapsing into Possibility

Collapsing into Possibility

Jerry Bradley

LITERARY PRESS
LAMAR UNIVERSITY

ISBN: 9781942956785
Library of Congress Control Number: 2020936354

Editor: Daniel Valdez

Lamar University Literary Press
Beaumont, Texas

Acknowledgments

The author gratefully acknowledges the following publications in which versions of these poems appeared:

Badlands: "Lovers in Parting"

Caesura: "The Carnival at Night"

Cape Rock: "The Roller Coaster Salesman's Lament"

CCTE Studies: "Against All Evidence," "Approaching the Coast of Arizona," "Bar Talk," "Bottleneck on I-10," "A Durable Measure," "The Hammer," "If I Had My Way," "Omar Khayyam at the Airport," "Still It Moves"

Di-vêrsé-city Anthology 2017: "Alive in Captivity after the Flood"

Houston Poetry Fest: "The Sound of Water"

Langdon Review: "Confessing My Crimes," "Ode to Drunken Folly," "Secrets," "The Trick of Enclosed Spaces"

Parody: "Milton the Busboy Asks for Friday Off"

Pushing the Envelope: "Dear Neighbor"

Red River Review: "A Class Birthday," "Have You Heard the One," "Sonnet on Sewage"

San Pedro River Review: "Breaking Ground"

Scholarship and Creativity on Line: "Another Lesson in Humanity," "A Kind Invitation," "Rats and Rainwater," "Something Else To Chew On"

Visions International: "The Dog in the Party Hat"

Words in Concert: "Gymnopédie #1"

Writing Texas: "Biking on Sunday," "Briss and Buttons," "Days After," "Days Before," "Don't Tell the Stars," "Fireworks at Halloween," "Hitcher," "Irony," "A Lot Like Chicken," "Lunch at the Great Wall," "Mixed Signals of Cause-and-Effect," "A Modern Moral," "Permanent Record," "A Second Grade Performance," "Self-Portrait," "The Small Birds of Bluffton," "Some Say," "Strewn Kisses," "Thirty Minutes In," "Thoreau Bread," "Unsolved Arkansas," "The Voluptuary," "Who Said," "A Year Later"

Recent Poetry from Lamar University Literary Press

Lisa Adams, *Xuai*

Bobby Aldridge, *An Affair of the Stilled Heart*

Charles Behlen, *Failing Heaven*

Mark Busby, *Through Our Times*

Julie Chappell, *Mad Habits of a Life*

Stan Crawford, *Resisting Gravity*

Glover Davis, *My Cap of Darkness*

William Virgil Davis, *The Bones Poems*

Jeffrey DeLotto, *Voices Writ in Sand*

Chris Ellery, *Elder Tree*

Dede Fox, *On Wings of Silence*

Alan Gann, *That's Entertainment*

Larry Griffin, *Cedar Plums*

Michelle Hartman, *Irony and Irrelevance*

Katherine Hoerth, *Goddess Wears Cowboy Boots*

Michael Jennings, *Crossings: A Record of Travel*

Gretchen Johnson, *A Trip Through Downer, Minnesota*

Betsy Joseph, *Only So Many Autumns*

Ulf Kirchdorfer, *Chewing Green Leaves*

Jim McGarrah, *A Balancing Act*

J. Pittman McGehee, *Nod of Knowing*

John Milkereit, *Drive the World in a Taxicab*

Erin Murphy, *Ancilla*

Laurence Musgrove, *Bluebonnet Sutras*

Benjamin Myers, *Black Sunday*

Godspower Oboido, *Wandering Feet on Pebbled Shores*

Jan Seale, *The Parkinson Poems*

Steven Schroeder, *the moon, not the finger, pointing*

Glen Sorestad, *Hazards of Eden*

Vincent Spina, *The Sumptuous Hills of Gulfport*

W.K. Stratton, *Colo-State-Pen: 18456*

Gary Swaim, *Quixotic Notions*

Wally Swist, *Invocation*

Ken Waldman, *Sports Page*

Loretta, Diane *Walker, Ode to My Mother's Voice*

Dan Williams, *Past Purgatory, a Distant Paradise*

Jonas Zdanys, *The Angled Road*

For information on these and other Lamar University Literary Press books go to www.Lamar.edu/literarypress

CONTENTS

A Little on the Small Side

Alive in Captivity after the Flood

Voluptuaries

Midway Down the Midway

Bad Role Models

A Little on the Small Side

Breaking Ground

Flat-chested as West Texas, the girls caravanned to the coliseum
to see Elvis, passing acres of chopped cotton and gas pumps
that stood like one-armed veterans a decade after the war.
Billboards hawked cheap rooms, tractors, used furniture,
but their engines purred like housecats all the way.

The moon on the horizon was as ripe as a peach and just as full,
but even then it was old-fashioned to trust things you could see.
No longer ensorcelled by the browns surrounding them,
they sought transformation in omens from a rockabilly boy
with sideburns, and that night they stared at the truth
until they could no longer see: the spectacle of a warmup trio
led by a boy with T. J. Eckleburg eyes, a rock-and-roll hammer
ready like God to break Lubbock's hardest heart.

Four years later his plane and career were victims of hapless gravity.
The girls, back in their homes, had turned boyfriends
into husbands and were already fashioning new lies.
What museum records their sadness now? Beneath
the billboards and floorboards, who furrows those fields,
that dirt that no one can ever quite leave behind?

A Second Grade Performance

On the proscenium I spoke as Jack Frost,
the imp who brings winter to the forest,
enunciating each word carefully and loud enough
to reach the cafetorium's back row.

Though my heart raced like a locomotive,
I was the freight my body lugged
toward horizons I had never dreamt.
Backstage I clung tightly to an iron pipe

and, when the curtain reopened, refused
to go back out. Someone else
would have to do my killing for me.
Between the tracks suicidal flowers grew.

A Lot Like Chicken

Hotter than two-dollar pistols, we stop
at the roadside park where Geronimo surrendered
and take a pull from the thermos. Like him we eat
on the run from open bags of carrots and celery
we packed for the road. And of course chicken—
wings and legs and thighs, one leftover breast,
and a small tub of livers.
                              I swear I've eaten more livers
than Jim Beam, but leaving Arizona I understand
why the old chief surrendered; the name says it all.
What could thrive under the bootheel of New Mexico?
Even cattle drives foundered in Skeleton Canyon.

But like him we have miles at our backs with more to go,
so it's on to Rodeo and the World's Largest Rattlesnake Rattle.
But take it from the Apaches: roadkill tastes a lot like hawk.

The Sound of Water

you know the sounds
water makes:
the drip of the tap

the patter of rain
and the crash of waves
on rocks

the thunder
of the cataract
that impresses honeymooners

the trickle of streams
the splatter of a shower
in a tub

how it sometimes
hammers its code
through old pipes

or calls to us
to relax and release
urinate

and if you listen
you can hear
the hum inside the water

how in the teakettle
it becomes steam
and curls like smoke

as it gropes for words
until it learns the tune
and finally begins to whistle along

Fireworks at Halloween

Like overgrown ivy, the starbursts twine
in the sky, then fall dark.
They amuse a ghoul in a blue Power Ranger suit
and his sister, a princess, who carries
a scepter and wears pink shoes.

They both like candy, want to grow up unkillable,
unafraid of all these powder-and-flash distractions.
But they too are spent rockets, shells without bullets.

Only in our imagination will the stars surrender.
Though every challenger may wing upward full of color,
it falls back without its fiery red and blue. Some strike
like copperheads; others cry like muezzins as they go.

And with bags half-full, they head down the block
where, as it suits, neighbors will answer or not.
I leave the light on fearing no one else will.

Approaching the Coast of Arizona

Kerouacing through West Texas, we pass miles
of tessellated farms, some with cotton,
some with summer hay. We bunk with friends
when we can—though they've always been too far between—
and collapse into possibility onto cots and old mattresses
like Schrödinger's cat, every bit alive but dead from the road.

One afternoon we took relief under trees
behind an elementary school where weeks before
kids had pledged themselves to a wall, until a colony
of flannel moths drove us back to the pavement.

Days later in a shinnery near the caprock, we lay
beneath the ellipsis of Orion's belt and let go.
The universe seemed to let go too, and the planets
delayed their appointed rounds. But our lives
have always been like that: a little on the small side.

No hope across the border either: the Jornado del Muerto,
Smokey's burial mound, the Bisti Badlands, Billy the Kid's grave,
and old Lincoln where the Grey Fox beat cancer with a bullet.
Beyond, California is already sinking into the sea.

Confessing My Crimes

the first thing I stole
was a plum
and God looked the other way

then I stood at the corner
where four roads met
and took the wrong one

while others scurried by
like measled rats headed
for the best bocconcini

I took it for the same reason
I burned an ex-lover's bed: to see
flames leap up and clap their hands

I did it for all the times
God stabbed me in the back
and I looked the other way

today across the fenceless pasture
I hear the birds speak
in dialects I cannot name

their breasts swell
like rainclouds promising a river
that never comes

their cries threaten
too late, too late
as if my revenge will not keep

and they speak of a betrayal
I have already tasted but cannot say
but unlike the birds

I can identify my accomplices
and I am ready to call them out
I am ready to name names

Against All Evidence

We share the morning's intimacies
while outside the chickens
flap and stretch in the early sun.

Then we rise and fold the quilt,
closing it like a book
and straightening its soft pages.

All night we were as silent
as birds on the breeze,
sleeping back to back with the patience

available mostly to the dead. But
this morning our dreams have left us
stranded, speechless, still in love,

but unable to say just how
wonderful it is to waken
with neither of us angry.

Bar Talk

Another crowded Friday with the band underway,
the clang of someone's top forty wrung from cymbals and snare,
and the surge of guitars contending for dominance
while an electric keyboard imitates cowbells, a flute, then a trumpet's blare.
Away from the dance floor, I hear the mythic tales of drunks
crowding the rail, dissonant harmonies of seduction and rebuke.
A woman presses close against me, turns with a smile.
"I think she's flirting," I tell my friend close by who can barely hear.
"How do you know?" he yells. "Listen to what she said," I say,
but again I have missed it by a quarter-mile.

Bars, like many spaces, offer proof that epiphanies are no fun,
but they are certainly a place to grow wise.
She said it was so crowded she could tell I'd been snipped.
But my hearing's as shot as my ego now:
I could have sworn she said *circus-sized*.

Work Detail in Louisiana

The grasses, mostly parchment, succumb
to their scythes as, magnetic and bent north,
they clean the ditches and harvest litter from the roadside.
They too have been called trash, near carbon copies
of one another in their orange jumpsuits and black skins.

Though hardly pedestrian, they are afoot
and harder than consonants.
Dad tells us to keep the windows shut.
"Not everyone can be cured,"
he adds, "by serving hard time."

But then, as if summoned, a billboard
announces the Boudain Hut at the next exit,
its motto boasting "we cure hunger."
In the closed car, our watering mouths
conjure whiffs of smoldering fat.

My old man was a barbecue recidivist. Ulcers
and a complaining GPS couldn't stop him;
he tried to go straight, but smoked meat
was his lodestone. And he knew how the taste
of retribution rode on every offender's tongue.

He reckoned we all would have to pay for our misdeeds
in time, and he could be as hard as any brisket's burnt end.
But some things really do seem to be in the blood.
Sharing a good meal, for instance, might bring people together
or make everyone brothers under the skin.

The Dog in the Party Hat

The final bucardo died in Spain,
the gastric brooding frogs are all gone,
the last wild passenger pigeon was killed by a BB gun,
and today you send birthday wishes:
a card with a dog in a red hat.

My birthday wish is that ages from now
that card and you survive, still beautiful
and waxing with hope like that lone prairie chicken
in a glass case at Harvard. May our years together
be a dog's life and every desire last seven years.

Permanent Record

Going through my mother's things, we spotted
a folder filled with papers saved from school:
certificates and ribbons, a few unframed awards,
a school supply list from junior high, shot records,
and a nearly-complete collection of report cards.

My grades were good, but my brother's and sister's
were as well. It was one of the unwritten family rules,
but sometimes my conduct was short of ideal.
There on one my teacher had inked too free with fists.

Undersized in third grade, I tried to make my way
in a new school, but I was too ashamed
to have my sister win my battles for me.
Still there were situations my hands couldn't resist.

It's been a good life since, though one way too full of punks
ready to throw a punch in a bar or a pick-up game,
even at the DMV once. Mostly I've tried to stand back,
but occasionally, even now, I find myself wanting to swing away.

But I was grown before I read that card,
way too late for that lesson learnt,
and what did my teacher know although
her judgment haunts me like an old song?
That card should have been burnt.

Every time I fought it was because I had to—
and has been all along—but my fists were never free.
Sometimes I won; sometimes I lost.
But every time I used them, it cost.

Lunch at the Great Wall

the man's cry melting from the ice that summer frightened the sherbet-eaters off the
terrace
    —Howard Nemerov, "The Icehouse in Summer"

Fattened on cashew chicken and some kind of noodle,
we rediscover ourselves in the Chinese zodiac—
she a snake and I a rat—and settle into the red-and-black
upholstery to face the replica faux-golden gong.

There is more than enough to eat, so we do,
thinking of dessert, perhaps something cold later on the patio,
always expecting something more, even after our singular fortunes
have been read: "Sometimes you happy, sometimes you sad."
At the register the prosperity cat waves his one-armed goodbye.

Wednesday

The morning paper reports its catastrophes
from around the world: another dead climber
on Everest, a sunken ferry in Congo
with more than a hundred still missing, plus
the corpse of a migrant child to add to the border's sum.

A lot of the truth isn't fit to repeat,
and, when the paperboy drives my street,
I wonder if he recognizes that all the white lines
are broken. Every sign hints that it's later
than we think, but many of us are not thinking.

And no matter how you score it, it is
a lot of dead people for a weekday.
And a safe place to land is always
in the mind of flying birds.

Unsolved Arkansas

In West Memphis the gangs still collide
in open warfare. Captains on each corner
study the breeze, count everybody's steps,
parp threats to the neighborhood.

You say the whole town is afraid at night,
blame the poverty, the buildings
and their dilapidation. But the watchtowers
in this city were never abandoned.

You say this place cries for change,
but there aren't two cents of hope left to rub together.
We must blame ourselves for our own delusions,
but we've grown numb like a tooth that's lost its nerve

but still wants to bite its own cheek.
That makes it hard to whistle
on these streets. Just don't blame the place—
or the bricks. Unlike us they've learned how to wait.

Biking on Sunday

Unstable as a juke joint, my knees
push me past the creaky roadhouse outside the city limit
where cars left over from Saturday's hookups loiter,
their fenders bartled with splashes of mud.

Apparently at the Tally-Ho they still hunt foxes
though the times I was there
I left alone and higher than a bitcoin.
It was like I'd opened a box of animal crackers
and found only missionaries inside.

But we should bless those entwined lovers
who may be learning this morning
how slow kisses make love last longer.
That's what I imagine as I pedal away
until I see the bumper sticker that reads
Stupid me: 20,000 battered women
and I've been eating mine plain.

The Hat on the Bed

It's bad luck to be superstitious!
                    —Finian McLonergan to Og, the leprechaun

You've had your share of superstitions,
the ones about spilled salt and the graveyards
you've whistled your way past, been careful
of Fridays and black cats, kept rabbits' feet
as jujus, even knocked on wood.

You've searched for clover under horseshoes,
nailed garlic above the door, avoided cracks
to spare your mother's sagging spine,
and eaten pecks of apples praying for
moments alone with the doctor's curvy wife.

But the pot of gold never scratched your palm;
all your pennies were found face down.
What was it then that cast a shadow on your grave?
Who put his shoes on the table
after the cake's candles were lit?

When the mirror of your life cracks
like a wishbone or the radii of an old umbrella
mistakenly opened inside, you can rub your eyes
with a disused wedding band if you like—
or until the dog howls or you finally see the light.

But when your nose itches, there's no need to wonder
who's coming. Call it beginner's luck, but you know
something inevitable is already on its way, one foot
heavy in front of the other. You can count its steps,
though you'll never likely hear the last shoe readying itself to drop.

Lovers in Parting

it is best to leave like this
when the earth is as still
and sleepy as an astronomer

and the bees have not yet begun to thrum
and ride in their soft petal saddles
as we did remembering our soundless first kiss

how we hid in the hayfield where the sun rose
and the wildflowers made faces behind our backs
as if trying to recall an old song

where the skeezix plodded twice in the shallow pond
before tearing across the pasture of goldenrod
his hoofprints flooding and filling behind him

but memories are an old constellation like the spokes
of a wagon wheel that radiate beyond the long grass
where they lie after rolling half-way around the world

it is not the stars that changed
we chose to blossom
where we now hang our tears in the trees

tomorrow the sun will be on its own

Public Notice

Our city wants to pass an ordinance
against heartbreak, mandate trigger warnings
in case the truth bow and invite us to dance
while poor Cinderella stays home ironing.
Voting yes changes little and will not save
our hardworking discalced maidens.

We should all second guess the taste of slop,
of cheese in the trap. And how many other Edens
will we plunder, pillage, clearcut, and ruin?
Must we count each step and study the breeze
before speaking our pledges toward the sorrowful moon?
When the line snaps tight and brings us to our knees,
the words we utter won't likely be clever beyond conjecture—
as if our birds could sing anything but scripture.

A Sonnet on Sewage

On the way home from ball practice,
my mother's station wagon fell in
behind the cesspool cleaner's truck.
I could see the gauge as she slowed to 28;

acres of mesquite and prickly-pear cactus
went by. Then I saw her grin,
wondering what it was about the muck
that tickled her so. It was a short wait.

The honeywagon was large and likely full of turds and piss;
it was the color of crap or a farmworker's skin.
Of course we couldn't see all the guck
inside, but there painted just above the plate

was as vile a word as I'd ever heard my mother utter:
Your shit is my bread and butter.

Who Said

I groan for the present sorrow, I groan for the sorrow to come.
        —Aeschylus, Prometheus Bound

Who said there was nothing in this town for an ugly woman to do?
They all seem taken in this bar. The blonde four stools down
has her attention on one of the lords of misrule who left his cycle
in the handicap slot and brags that his sofa may pull out
but he won't. His pledges on the bathroom wall affirm
the old dictum: what makes us long makes us strong.

Even the barmaid is as fresh as a fossil: the abortuary between her legs
is dark enough to make Rothko smile. But I'm drunker than Kit Marlowe
in the Bull House, and I tip every beer just to watch her curtsy like a circus bear.

She looks like she's dying faster than I am—and I'm dying faster than I want.
But we're all afraid of ending up alone like dead cars along the roadside.
Our longings can convey us only so far, even when Cupid seems
an open-carry vigilante ready to shoot up the whole town tonight. I want to go
like a meteor that never hits ground, not hauled down the hallway by my heels.

Still, if you're looking for a shameless evening, this may be your kind of place.
That faded poster behind the bar, just like us, used to be something.

If I Had My Way

she said falling in love
was like falling up
into the clouds

though I said it was more like
putting my hands
under her sweater

and feeling her breasts flower
into buds like the ones that grew
in the garden where we first kissed

and I hoped to prove my point
but according to her
I was confusing love and sex

I knew about them
the birds and bees
because I'd seen them do it

well, not the bees
most of whom never mate
but die dedicated nonetheless

gazing through adoring
compound eyes (though none
so blue and lucent as hers)

and I told her
I was like them
the bees

and I was ready to love her
until we too could make honey
in the lion's head

Have You Heard the One

a man does not walk into a bar
and will not see the patron
with the duck under his arm
so there is no joke
and neither comes to harm

in another a guy cannot drive
but still will not ask
his neighbor for a ride
nor borrow his mower
or his nymphomanic wife

a third may deign
to ask directions
of the farmer down the lane
and thereby safely travel
unfamiliar terrain

then there's the man on a date
who refuses
to play doctor with his mate
he feels just fine
and cannot abide the hour's wait

the talking dog however rubs his collar
and chases happiness like a car
his lips unbutton with each swallow
and though a thousand punchlines mislead
he refuses to say just when the leash got smaller

Instructions for Staying in Your Room

Ill at ease in a new city, you turn on the television
whose first channel always reminds that you are welcome
(as are all conventioneers) to be here, to dine
in the rooftop restaurant, and to drink in its glittering bar—
or in your room should that prove more convenient.
Above all you should make yourself comfortable.
The staff remains ready to assist you with every need.

And stay safe. You are requested to keep your door locked
with the chain affixed. You must not open it for strangers.
You should call the front desk to confirm the arrival
of hotel employees who may drop in to silence
the heater's ceaseless tap or tend a heedless drip.
Perhaps you should not leave the premises at all
(especially since the city unfolds so majestically
from the sky terrace twelve stories above), but, if you do,
leave your valuables in the complementary safe
and be mindful of your surroundings. Do not speak
to strangers (as if you might see anyone else).

And should you smell smoke, place a wet towel
against the door and close the curtains. Do not
attempt to leave your room and certainly do not
ride the elevator. Please do as you are told. Help
is already on the way. Hear those sirens outside?
They may be coming for you. Rest assured everyone
will be rescued in time. Until then you must sit and await
further instruction, as if it had never occurred to you
just how hard it is to come so far only to have to stay put.

Old Time Religion

People brag about the poverty they grew up in,
the hardships they overcame, the overbearing fathers
quick to wield a belt but to whom now in adulthood
they proudly attribute their own smug rectitude.
It is, they say, the way of Solomon the wise,
this spare-the-rod thing, although Rehoboam
might have offered a different opinion on the matter.

Let's not speak of satire, for those who misread
a proverb may also mistake a shepherd's crook
for a club. But what if we're all too quick to temper?
And why is it violence seldom gets lost in translation?

So let's play *what if*. The adage doesn't say
if we spoil the child. So what if we spare the *if*?
"Oh, but it's implied," they insist. "The *if*
is understood, although it be as invisible as God.
This is the way the wise among us regulate conduct."

Well, here's an implication for you. What if the lines
aren't an epigram but a commandment? What if
we parse its bossy grammar, its imperious call,
and obey the necessity to both love our children
and spoil them as well? *If* indeed.

Extending the Metaphor

a beautiful woman
is a fine instrument,
like a piano

and if she's not upright,
she's bound to be grand

Alive in Captivity after the Flood

Alive in Captivity after the Flood

The first thing I ask of any environment is that it should be ignoble.
　　　　—Philip Larkin

There are lots of ways to be blind,
but you can smell water
even when you can't read a map:
volcanic beachheads, a wild trench,
ambiguous lines of terrain,
each divided by the transitive property of water.

Admire the math of a cornfield maze,
the farmer who dusts his hands
in fulfillment while the silo leans forward
as if it has something to say.
Beyond it, tamed and peaceful,
a disused church stands, its eyes
broken like the last panes of heaven.

You've seen this, and through birthday binoculars
you've seen other scapes: ructions at the waterhole
in a world so flat that everything seems in view—
hyenas, vultures, herds of elegant ungulates.

Home it's all possumhaw and crawdad palace.
I like the land, animals, birds, this place;
still I wonder what it wants me to know.
So I listen when the water speaks;
I look when it tells me to,
but mostly I go when it says go.

Mixed Signals of Cause-and-Effect

My block gathers on the driveway
of my righteous neighbor to help him load
the last cases of water into his motorhome.
The time to decide is now upon the rest of us:
the roads west are already closed; the Gulf lies
to the south; if we head east, the storm
will chase us through the shoulderless roads
of Louisiana. So it's either head north or stay put.

We exchange phone numbers as if
we mean to stay in touch, though
we won't be much help to one another
once Harvey's here. "Don't worry.
God will provide," he says, as he lifts
his bichon into the passenger seat.
"He always does."

He is so confident of his claim that
he doesn't even offer anyone else a ride out,
although none of us would care to go
with him all the way to Lubbock.
And his proclamation leaves me speechless—
or almost. Why is he packing
if he's one of the ones God intends
to protect? Or is one of them bluffing?

Good folks have lost it all in Rockport
and Port Aransas. I've seen them on tv
pining over furniture, family, and pets.
Montgomery seems next for a direct hit,
and we are in line to follow.

Even my plainspoken insurance carrier
calls this an act of God, but my neighbor
sees only dark blessings ahead.
I don't know if God is determined
to kill us all, but his threat does seem pretty serious.
And how will we know until after the deed is done?

I tell him to remember that there are two kinds
of snakes in Texas—poisonous and non-poisonous—
and everyone who dies of snakebite
was bitten by a venomous one.

My claim puzzles him.
"How could we know?"
Well, he wouldn't have died if it weren't,
I say. My fallacy is just like his view of God:
circular and coiling on a narrow axis.
The answer begs all our questions.

"Huh," he grunts, shifting his position
behind the wheel and twisting the key.
And as he pulls away, we wave to each other,
not knowing if we'll see each other again,
but both of us seem so ready to leave Old Eden.

Days Before

Beaumont is broiling, and summer's only half done.
Heat rises in waves off the concrete like Calypso's ardor
and tries to lure us inside, but it's too hot even for oysters to mate.

In the trainyard a hoodoo rat with a spray can
has painted a bloody sunrise on a boxcar
and dogs show us their tongue
as if we were doctors. Their skin changes
like a thermochromic crystal with a fever,
and the birds skriking for water will soon have their wish.

We say that life is too long to drink short beer.
And, besides, what is it we haven't said about the weather
to the pour man at the bar who replenishes our drinks.
Someone is always eager to complain, to joke
about the forecasts of two-foot rain.

Double it for all I care one says. Another
regrets having not photographed the last deluge.
Other things that could go without saying don't.
We just can't imagine how the whole county
will soon be cowbellied in the river's soft mud.

But at closing time we'll rise and go back
into the night, blinking as if there were still time
to absorb the stars—or something closer.
After all, what counts most is what we learn
after we already know everything else.

Hitcher

The rain rolls in from the west; no,
it limps like a stodgy hitchhiker,
an old man you might pick up
beside the road. And once

he's settled in, he'll likely begin
to tell you all his secrets.
And, since the road is slow,
he'll tell them a second time as well,

flooding your ears little by little
until in time the whole car
will be awash with wet lies.
Harvey was like that. You knew

you'd have way more hours with him
than you wanted, at times wondering
when he might come up for air
or if his turtle neck would ever

draw back into his dwingey suit
to retrieve more accounts of the misery
he's known. But, heck, you've seen
enough of that on your own. Hear how

the rain picks up a little? It's just
him reminding you that you're a pair,
the two of you in this together
all the way for a very long ride.

Rats and Rainwater

The week India came to Texas,
nothing stirred except rats and rainwater.
They teemed from gutters and overran dry spaces
while we huddled like Hindus in our houses,
electricity down, hoping the tv
might reincarnate itself at any moment.

Told to prepare for fifteen inches—
not fifty—we wondered what the gods
might unleash. South of here,
ranchers cut their fences, freeing
Brahmas to seek higher ground.

We've seen them along the roads,
plodging through the flood
or straddling the white line;
like ancient wise men they shake
their heavy dewlaps in disbelief.
All our sacred cows are running loose.

Something Else To Chew On

The motels and cafes are closed
along the only open route. There is no gas.
I might as well stay here and stand in line
with thousands to beg for the last loaf of bread.

A case of water is ten dollars,
but what rises over the baseboards
and collects in the carpet pads is free.
The cell phone predicts more is on the way.

Though I have mastered the technique
of grilling pot pies, the food in the freezer
is thawing faster than I can eat.
Survival can be hard on the stomach

though soon enough we'll have charity forced
down our throats, something else for us to chew on.

Briss and Buttons

Now that the tv's out
I have time to clean the drawers
and am astounded I have
held on to so much that is old fashioned.

Who knows who first owned these relics—
these bobbins and combs, ornaments,
curios, all these tranklements
of unremembered lives that lie now
like unredeemed coupons
once full of good intentions.

As I ratch through the debris,
I set a few things aside,
then skifte the drawer bottoms.

Dust and fluff fall like snow
on ceramic swans, ancient cobwebs spun
by the spider who lives in my house,
or more probably a sleepwalking woman
or someone long dead.

This flood like all tragedy
teaches us to believe in death again,
the power and futility of it all.

We shall wear our graveclothes
for eternity, our split jackets,
no shoes on our feet,

but these simple dead things,
tiny as they are, remind
that at one time we were essentially alive

and what we've hung onto,
all these diminutives,
won't delay infinity one whit.

Don't Tell the Stars

no one tells the stars
when to shine

though curfew's at ten
a group of teens
goes by afterward
with a pack of tall-boys
in the seat

the driver honks
and gives me
the one-finger Texas wave

see you in the movies
he shouts
and perhaps one day
he will

because who knows where
we're all headed
but wherever it is
I promise not to tell the stars

Strewn Kisses

Harvey passes out wet kisses to everyone,
but he won't stay. We know his kind,
fickle as a two-dollar knife,
and we'll be glad to see him go, but
it's the sense of loss we'll never get used to.

He'll leave his footprints in the mud
we've grawded into our carpets. And though
we may summon memories of poor Job
and how he prospered again, we won't
be the same after we rebuild.
Dark channels course through our heads
the same way black bayous filled our town.

Though the flood wasn't quite biblical, from all reports
Harvey held everyone a little too close, lingered
just a bit too long. We didn't know when he'd leave,
just that he would. And we knew he wouldn't do that
until he'd chased the very last angel out of the bottomland.

Days After

The salvage crews and water have done their job:
refrigerators that stood like toll booths at the curb
have now been hauled away and clog the sloughs,
swamps, and bayous where like goliaths
cotted in the downed branches they snicker
in a minor key at the nicker of water on rocks.

Beaumont's soggy letter to the Gulf
just got longer, though it did open
its arms wide for our debris.
And the refractory grandchildren
who were dandled through the storm
have forgotten their unanswered pleas to God,
though the oldest recall how
they have been baptized by running water
more than once already.

This is surely paradise in reverse,
creation without wishclouds to dream on,
no pond ice or waterfalls, no willows
left to strum the surge like David's harp.

But there will be new roofs and floors
and temporary trailers sitting side-by-side
with barely a squinch between.
And when the restaurants re-open,
we'll gather there to exchange our tales
of hardship. And then the freedom to be
miserable will make us all happy once again.

A Kind Invitation

This morning my neighbor crosses over
to invite me for coffee made from pool water.
He'll boil it, he says, plus the chlorine
should help. He notices my demurral.

I offer in jest to sharpen sticks
for rat kebabs or bring a can of fruit cocktail,
because all of us suspect that soon enough
everyone will be defecating in the woods with gators.

He senses my reluctance, adds,
"I haven't peed in it, you know."
I believe him—but I do
know someone who has.

Another Lesson in Humility

The power's back on, and we forsake the DVR
to tune in live reports from nearby places with faraway names—
Nome, China—and witness repeated rooftop rescues,
people in nursing homes sitting in lap-deep water,
lost pets, and driverless cars floating down bayous.

A local correspondent reports from a deluged field
where the flood threatens a major artery.
She hears—we all hear—two voices calling
from the tree line. She flags down two men
in a pickup pulling a johnboat. Moments later
mid-broadcast the first one is in it and ferried to the road.

Safe, he tells her they have been in the trees
since four this morning, more than six hours,
and he shivers audibly as we watch his friend
descend his perch and grasp for the beer-cooler preserver
the men keep tossing. Each throw snags in the brush.
"Swim for it," they finally say. And he does.

When they drag him into the boat, we see
he is not wearing pants. He covers his face
with a loaned jacket and declines to give his name
or speak on the air. Unoffered explanations
wash over us like waves: Did he shuck his jeans
from the weight of the water? Was his
underwear swept away too? Or more likely,
had it been just another Saturday night
that ended with him wearing nothing at all?

Irony

—for Ken Meisel

I once lived in Socorro, a town
that despite its name offered
little help—few restaurants,
not much medical care—a place where we
sometimes spoke different languages.
Everyone knew he was pretty much on his own.

Many of the town's daughters were called
Linda and Celia and Bonita as if their parents
hoped one day they might grow
into the beauty of their names.

So when Harvey hit Beaumont, I looked
for higher ground, that beautiful mountain
promised by its name. But I was just another
whitebreader who'd again been swindled
by a misleading label, and I wondered if somewhere
another traveler was wearing my name.

A Year Later

one year later
the water is no more
reflective than I am

but I do tread with a lighter step—
like the doomed cat
who strolls knowingly
beneath the hawk on a low branch

however there is no raptor rehab
in this town and providence
is always fleeting

the cemetery is full
of failed prescriptions
and we can see exactly
what our jimmycrack ideas
have come to

instead of reading
about drownings
we now hear about
bar shootings in Mexico
the danger has moved on

but there is still
heartbreak in the machine
even after the Coke-man
opens its chest
and removes the leaky can

the Dow hits new highs
and somewhere someone
is cloning a mastodon
leaving the rest of us
a kind of moveable bull's eye
with nothing left to resort to
except common life

Voluptuaries

The Voluptuary

It is time not sun
    that melts the snowman
        and suspends our expectations;

like an armless clock
    it watches its own beginning end
        as the sun climbs by degrees

through our generation
    before lapsing into
        the predicament of boredom.

If we were in the middle
    of something that mattered,
        the sky might mend,

and we could throw away
    hat and carrot,
        our hard eyes of coal,

and, faceless nothings,
    face the nothing
        that grows gradually wider

until we find ourselves at last
    holding a dusty broom
        beneath the silent falling snow.

Christening the Rod

And he looked up, and said, I see men as trees, walking.
        —Mark 8:24

Christening the new rod,
I hold the tip low to the water
and strip the line with my forefinger.

I cast upstream toward the canopy
of a large cottonwood and watch the line drift,
the fly glide along the water's glassy top.

In a knee-deep swale
I tease the brown, both of us
looking for an easy meal.

When at last he strikes, I bow,
give him some slack, and follow
as he steers me downriver.

I tip him away from reeds
and logs until my dark glasses
spot him through the glare.

Then I scoop him into the net
and point his eyes to the sky
as I cut slowly along the belly,

inserting my knife into a gill
and pressing outward toward the head.
With cold thermos water I wash away

the entrails and blood. Fileted, he opens
like a bible. Then I dislodge the eyes,
freeing him like Jesus again to walk upon water.

Some Say

Some say the world will end in ice
on a patio or sunny veranda,
cooling a glass of artillery punch
surrounded by blooming jacaranda.

Others say that fire will do the trick
if we keep the cooker lighted,
with whiffs of charring meat about
to keep our hearts delighted.

It's hard to know how the world might go
when viewed from a reclining chair.
Why bother with how long we've got?
Best not to even go there.

And who has time to perish twice,
and who would make that choice?
So let me freshen up your glass
with a little Clos du Bois.

Secrets

Only ashes can keep a secret.
            —Ramón Gómez de la Serna

What lovely things trees become—
boats and billboards, birdhouses,

the longest love letter penned by hand.
Portraits smudged in charcoal,

papier mâché masks. Perhaps even
a loveseat where an enamored one

may recline to pluck a stringed
instrument. Sometimes

a tree resembles an abandoned bracelet,
its many circles bangling into blossom.

The hearts of beeches pulse deep
in the bottomland; their wood burns

clean and evenly except when there is
a twist in the grain. Lust is that kind of twist.

It smolders in secret, often unable
even to hold its own tongue.

Self-Portrait

if I could, I would paint my skull
in some sort of crown

like an archbishop
regal, imperial

a chess piece adorned
with ribbons and garland

my scepter would be an axe
that prunes away dead years

but my eyes have already dimmed to nuance
my hands are too unsteady for detail

and my brain so far from my toes
loses count of my steps

even my face has outlasted
its mirror image

so any rendering of me now
would show a modest painter

one so old that even
his brushes are nearly bald

Cemetery Fire, Bastrop County

the week after the fire, survivors
    exhausted by the world

prepared for the next
    and cleaned the grounds

the row of oaks by the entry gate
    became firewood a second time

and mementos, so many flowers
    and toys, were destroyed

burned to the quick—
    but not the dead

though they too had their own taste of hell,
    one they had tried so long to avoid

Thirteen Ways of Looking at McCartney's "Blackbird"

I

Just three sounds: Paul's voice,
a Martin D-28, and his two feet
alternating in time.

II

The first barre is Bach's Bourrée,
an ancient foregleam in E minor,
a gavotte done to a lute.

III

On the White Album
the Beatles were no longer one band.
Paul sang by himself, double-tracking
his own vocal on the refrain.

IV

The birdsongs are not music,
just the calls of sparrows and finches
captured live outside Abbey Road.

V

The cut was the B-side
to George's gently weeping guitar.
The upside was someone
eventually turned it over.

VI

Blackbirds don't sing at night,
though Paul did once
to the Apple scruffs who waited
for him outside his London home.

VII

Poets are blackbirds
who in the dead of night
dream of being singers.

VIII

In Brown v. Board of Education,
the blackbirds of Central High
showed they knew how to rule the roost.

IX

Kafka is Czech for jackdaw,
a blackbird whose steps in the leaf-litter
can approximate human speech.

X

On a Tarantino-directed episode of ER,
Susan played "Blackbird" on a cassette
to calm Chloe during the delivery of her baby.

The next season, missing her niece,
she sang it to herself.

XI

A blackbird is a bad-luck totem,
part of the void at the core of creation.

But if you capture one in your dreams,
your misfortunes turn into success.

XII

To protest Michael Jackson's purchase
of the Beatles' catalog,
the Dandy Warhols waited until he died
to release their take.

They were only waiting
for their moment to arise.

XIII

At the Oscars, Dave Grohl
played it for the recent dead
as photos of Stan Freberg
and Leonard Nimoy rolled by.

"Musical bliss," he called it.

Bottleneck on I-10

Atop freezing rain
we slid into H-town

like an open chord
with the footfeed down

wary on each overpass
to note the careless and insane

who rollick across bridges
and into our slowly unthawing lane

You fingered your rosary
as if it were strings on a guitar

and the blues were the black driver
we'd paid to chauffeur our car

but then we always choose sad songs
when freak storms hit

and stammer toward the horizon
fretting every last mile of it

Dear Neighbor

We have spoken about the fire ants, and I hope
I am forgiven. You gave me something to think about,
and now and again, like today, I do. So let's let the old days
be done if only because spring is here at last and it is once again
the time of seed. We've both made another circle around the sun,
and soon the sticky tongue of summer will be on us all. And I will try
to heed the maxim to love my neighbor as myself, although life has taught
me that love can be a fine servant but is a tyrannical master.

I know we had words, but I didn't get to use all of mine.
Nor did I complain about the four turkeys you fattened at Thanksgiving
that found their way over your fence and onto my patio
where they stared at their reflections in the sliding door
every afternoon for a month, defecating incessantly.
Nor did I fault your leaving your driveway floodlights on all winter,
even though their brightness sneaked past my bedroom curtains, because,
well, ours is a rough neighborhood and somebody should leave them on.
And I know, I know my cats frequented your pansy bed far too often,
but did that really warrant your adopting Cerberus from the no-kill shelter?

But, if my cats can modify their behavior, I guess I can too. All
we need to know about life is that the liver is a regenerative organ
but the heart is not. That's an idea we both should raise a glass to.
And today we have the sun again, though later the sky will be full of stars,
and next year we will both fall to our knees dreaming tomatoes.

So what I ask is this: tonight when it's dark and far Arcturus beckons,
please pen your dog and douse your light. My long chair,
that yearly facsimile of hope, is already out and waiting,
and, when I'm home, I hope it, the darkness, and a tall glass
will work their magic. And I ask you for once to let me be
the gutshot cat who upon returning home gets the comfy chair.

The Trick of Enclosed Spaces

The neighbor's rosary grows westward
toward the foothills far away, but it's all illusion.
His garage doesn't descend to the stone wall;
it just seems to, the slope proving that, if we counted
each stride and the next as we paced among the floribundas,
the double-delights, and Mojave hybrids,
if we stepped from the miniatures to the polyanthas
and sank transit stakes in their clusters, we could refute our eyes.

But we won't because we like believing that all things
grow toward water. It is the low ground, not the high,
that entrances, and, when the sky is suitably dramatic,
its pronouncements intend to fool, so that what we see
in this gradient garden flattened by clouds
are merely flowers made oddly squarer
by the widening lines of masonry and wall.

If there were trees—and there could be—
there might also be angels or elves atop the rocks,
and, if there were a pond, a fish might fling its shadow
upon these petaling beds or brim like a goblet or flute,
a theodolite of champagne. We have metaphors
to counter such flatness.
                          But when night comes
and the outside shadows, taller than yesterday's,
creep up a wall brightened by blooms, we once again
calculate, derive our proofs, and call upon proverbs
to teach us what we already know: despite what goes
unseen in the dark, we often see so much less in the light.

The Small Birds of Bluffton

This is low country
    full of alligator driftwood
        and wandering tattlers

perching passerines,
    plovers, sanderlings,
        turnstones and swifts—

the kinds of things we thought
    vanished with the angels.
        On shore the flycatchers

tumble like acrobats
    in low clouds and drizzle
        to the wren's effervescent song.

It is hard not to love
    the larklike wagtails and pipits
        with their streaky plumage,

bushtits in their woven nests,
    longspurs and buntings
        shrikes, warblers, towhees

the sight of dark-eyed juncos
    winging toward drier ground,
        the itch of rain as it runs down your ear

A Durable Measure

Heaven's hand is not gentle, nor is earth's.
        It holds wide fears and disease, nailed windows,
            coffins for two, parasites and panderers
in wild revue. Cancer is always a shock,
        the teenager too with a crushed lung,
            and the resuscitant patient disallowed to die.
The hospice, an antique shop, sags
        like heavy furniture. The x-ray, no hope, does not lie.

In the next room a man with a bone brush
        braids a woman's hair. If you turn on your side,
            you can hear them whispering behind the wall
where other lovers and convalescents call.
        Their skins threaten to burst when they pray;
            the psalms, force-fed, are too loud,
as if the words have grown just too large to say.

Sniff the breeze below the mantelpiece,
        listen to the renter's cough as he opens the wine
            to breathe. The moon will inherit this jeweled box,
this House of Dissolution with upholstered seats;
        it holds the future like a tumor beneath her arm.
            See the way they shiver together,
how they cover themselves in darkness?
        Toast your open vein and at last begin to warm.

Still Life with Apples

In the photos
    of our wedding
        neither of us holds still,

each in a hurry
    to get to our future
        (as we are still).

And though the present
    keeps intruding, the world
        is the same world still,

and it turns as it must
    shaping desire around the axis
        of something remarkably still.

In an age of apples
    love is no longer forbidden,
        and it beckons to us still,

claiming that we live in
    what is just a world
        and nothing more—still

we should
    pause a moment
        while things are still,

before we are too old
    to reconstruct
        the scene and are still

able to recall not only
        what was but what
                might be still.

The fruit I taste
        on your lips tonight baffles
                as though it had been distilled

from a long life with apples—
        yet still a life and still ours,
                no matter now how implacably still.

December 20th

The almanac reminds that tomorrow's solstice
precedes the year's longest night,
though no one's wish will likely keep the storm away.
The sky may not be clear enough to see the falling star
sprinting toward us, but even our best hope seems
determined to snag itself on its long tail of light.

You should have been a woodcutter's wife; instead
we go to bed cold with part of each other's darkness within,
but in three months, when the sun comes back
across the equator, we'll try to re-enter the garden again.

We'll push aside the thornhedge and hollowed trees
and draw water in golden buckets. The finger
that doused tonight's flame will once again hold your hand.
Then I'll call myself a lucky fellow. But tonight
when I search for happiness, I'll carry an umbrella.

Thirty Minutes In

Thirty minutes in, and the stranger
next to me is already asleep
against my shoulder, snoring as if
he had boarded with no conscience.

There hasn't even been enough time
for the steward to bring the obligatory
pretzels and Diet Coke.

I count heads to distract myself
(more than a hundred with no vacant seats)
and wonder how many like me,
are headed to an indifferent city with no one
to greet them on the ground.

Surely some will be welcomed by a kiss
and a friendly embrace, but between arrivals
every trip breaks into fractions,
numbers so small they may not even matter.

It's my curse to tally travel's offenses,
to imagine the sadness of each tearful farewell,
while above us the same moon reflects
onto everyone's backyard, as if to promise
the next flight will not be short of seats.

Midway Down the Midway

The Hammer

common as pennies
    we ride the peen of the Hammer
downward to its target
    in our daring descent to bull's-eye earth

waving our arms
    and squealing like the bubble dancers
frying sopapillas just down the midway

giddy and out of control
    two twisting sky angels
chasing a teenage romance

the firmament, the land, the stars
    everything so close
all of it almost within reach

Chicken

Chicken is the only animal we eat before it's born and after it's dead.

In the food stalls it predominates, it's everywhere—
chicken in tacos, chicken on a stick,
wings in sauce and patties between bread,

or diced and wokked in bowls
(with skin and without), pickled eggs
in the beer tent and fried ones on burgers,

omelets for the brunch crowd,
even beaks and feet (you suspect)
in the chili, corndogs, and wieners,

and all those dark stains, splatters on the pavement,
each bearing foul witness to a gastrophobe's bad dream.
But you can't have it both ways; you are what you eat.

You can't fill up and ride the Tilt-a-Whirl, so take your pick.
What are you, chicken? she taunts when you shun
the Sea Dragon, your eyes swimming with each sway.

And you begin to think maybe you are:
your words catch in your craw
as you cock your head to one side

and scratch with your left foot in the dirt.
You can almost feel the pinfeathers
rasping against your shirt.

The Rollercoaster Salesman's Lament

What kind of person has a job like this?
    Seasonal, they said—
        but only if you can't make a sale.

Otherwise the weeks drag on
    until your tan no longer remembers
        how summer felt.

I knew enough not to sign on,
    but I needed another last chance.
        What do I know?

The only one I ever rode
    left me hungry for a month.

Reflecting Again

in the maze of the glass house
I see myself over and over
like every face snared by a mirror

but there are rules of reflection:
be careful where you step
and keep both eyes closed

because the way out looks
like the way in, like here,
like now, like me

and when you put one foot forward
you know the other
is readying to disappoint

and along these walls I feel
nothing more
than the desire to escape

unable to but hoping
that the distance holds
someone somewhere else

The Carnival at Night

When the Kreepy Kastle falls dead
and Pharaoh's Fury no longer parts the tide,
the games close with the biggest bears

on the bottom shelf still unwon
and the carnies, all but drunk, still joking
about how many ferrets it takes to power the wheel.

At night gravity returns to the Orbitron;
the calmed Dixie Twister lazes while the Dodgem cars
idle at the site of the last spinout. The Cliffhanger,

where we once sat in a cage terrified of the drop,
no longer dangles. And when the hum of generators slows,
one by one the lights go out until at last

we walk in full darkness, wringing our cotton-candied
hands as we watch the stars fall into place
with only the moon now to keep us awake.

Bad Role Models

A Modern Moral

Orpheus fell in love with Eurydice,
but just after their wedding
she was bitten by an adder and died.

Heartbroken, he went
to the underworld to bring her back
where he charmed Hades—though the head

of a king should never be turned by flattery,
particularly if his wife is a woman
accustomed to perpetual darkness.

So Persephone said, "You can have her back,
but you'll have to go back to the world
without looking to see if she is following behind."

Damned if he didn't almost make it,
but he weakened and turned around for her
as if she were Melania deplaning Air Force One.

He lost her forever and was left staring
at the again-visible stars, dumbstruck and befuddled,
just like a president staring wide-eyed at his own personal eclipse.

Still It Moves

I.

Galileo, that heliocentric heretic, was forced to recant
how Earth moves around the Sun, though he still knew more
about heavenly bodies than any archbishop could.
So when the Inquisitors threw him in prison—abjured, cursed, and detested—
he wrote "eppur si muove" on the dungeon wall. Or maybe he said it
as he stepped from home confinement, pointing to the firmament,
perhaps even stamping his foot upon the ground.

Or maybe he never said it but would have
had he seen that mini-skirted woman emerging from a taxi
in front of the Venetian Palace and climbing the corpse-white stairs
of the Wedding Cake to the colonnade. It was a rear that could make
even an astronomer go blind—which he eventually did—
but it wouldn't likely have killed him as the church threatened to do
though he did suffer palpitations, insomnia, a hernia, and fever.
One wonders what Italian beauties kept old Copernicus awake.

II.

The Altar of the Fatherland is a joke as big as the church.
Both honor kings. Above them lies the Capitoline Hill
where one Caesar crawled on his knees to appease his own god
and avert Jupiter's unlucky stare. Six months later
he was dead, and his assassins had locked themselves in the temple.
His crown and reputation, like objects dropped from a tower,
fell at the same rate, their descent independent of their mass.

Centuries later mononymous Galileo spied Jupiter's moons,
below which, as with our own, lovers ardently kiss
and discover new paradises. But his god divulged himself
only in numbers, in the precision of the vastest spaces,
and in those orbits where every celestial body would in time
come into view, even when seen from the backseat of a Fiat sedan.

III.

In a world where axiality and symmetry govern,
Galileo gave the finger to Aristotle and lived,
but he died like a saint, his body plundered,
its parts revered for their sacred power.

Now in a bell jar in Florence, his middle finger stands
upright with two others and a tooth under glass
in a museum devoted solely to instruments, where even a starlet
can take his measure—and her own—as new heavens pass by.

Damnatio Memoriae

Elagabalus, fourteen, was, the bastard son
   (his grandmother swore)
       of her nephew, Caracalla, murdered
on Turkish soil, a man without heir.
   Macrinus, the man behind the killing,
      was an equestrian prefect in the Praetorian Guard
who had himself proclaimed emperor.
   But his rule did not last,
      and history throttled forward.

Encouraged by bounties,
   soldiers killed Macrinus
      and named Elagabalus emperor.
He stayed in Syria for a year
     consolidating power
       before re-entering Rome
with his family who carried before them
   the image of Helios (his household god)
     struck from a large conical stone.

He reigned four years:
   there were no wars, roads got built, and
     he ceremoniously dispensed the treasury's wealth.
But he appointed actors, chariot drivers, and others
   to high positions based upon penis size
     rather than rank and ability.
Then he created a female version of the Senate.
   He was accused of favoritism, excessive luxury,
     sexual impropriety. He reveled in languor.

The marble statues he erected
    portray him soldierlike, though Elagabalus
        wore his hair long and dressed in strange
costumes from the East. He wore makeup
    and asked to have a vagina
        carved into his depilated flesh.
He smothered banquet guests under an avalanche
    of petals and prostituted himself, beckoned
        from palace doorways, naked as Caligula.

More serious were his offenses to religion.
    He abandoned his wife and broke other taboos:
        married the high priestess of the vestal virgins,
elevated himself to the pantheon, displacing Jupiter,
    and built a temple in which as priest-emperor
        he was worshiped above all others.
Then like other gods he was killed. The Praetorian Guard
    dragged his headless body through the streets
        before throwing it into the Tiber.

Elagabalus dreamt of new pleasures and impossible passions;
    he envied Nero for burning Rome. He wanted
        everything because everything disgusted him.
After his death his name was erased from inscriptions
    and papyri. What was left of him included
        only a few coins and some busts.
His younger cousin, a boy he had adopted
    (another of Caracalla's proclaimed bastards),
        succeeded him. Afterward everyone was bored.

Omar Khayyam at the Airport

the moving sidewalk moves
and having moved
moves on

as the ticket machine whirs its greeting
and prints his pass to board

he heads toward a distant gate
while faster pedestrians stream by

oh, who returns to tell of the roads
the lonely travelers fly?

earth cannot answer
nor the seas mourn

but the moving sidewalk moves
and having moved
moves on

until at last it yields
to open concourse

where as he trudges
his wheeled suitcase cracks a heel

and he limps past bootblacks
newsstands and an overpriced florist

before sidling aboard again
exhaling loudly as he emerges

as the moving sidewalk moves
and having moved
again moves on

Milton the Busboy Asks for Friday Off

When I consider how the light bill was spent,
the sum for groceries, and have for six months lied
outright about cadging loose tips on the side,
it seems pointless, doubly so when I am skint,
to miss a day at this sorry restaurant.
Ungrateful though the owner is, curse his hide,
ready to wrest his toll, my day off denied,
I ask politely anyway, stay patient
to his stinging reply: "Tony does not need
someone who will not work. Do what you think best:
bear your mild yoke, attend the dishes. Your nerve
is ungodly. Diners by the hundreds speed
here to eat, to sup, hurry to carve and rest.
They also wait who only stand and serve."

Ode to Drunken Folly

with apologies to John Keats

My head aches, and a blowzy dumbness pains
My gut, as though of Maalox I had drunk
Or emptied some toxin into my veins
This evening past and downwards numbdrunk sunk:
I thirsted despite all the good beer bought.
No longer giddy in feigned happiness,
I, once higher than the tall cuckoo'd trees,
Recall that reeling barstool where I sat
And played A-16 over and endless,
Singing loudly 'til I slid to my knees.

Thoreau Bread

Eating some indigestible loaf or pan-fried
bottom feeder, Henry probably
didn't realize how much he'd miss the future,
content as he was to be distracted by warring ants
and the teardrop bulbs of Dutchman's britches.

After your surgery my one wish
was for you to come back whole,
but deceiving what impends is harder
than throwing a surprise party
for a clairvoyant.

We are constantly encouraged to think outside
some imaginary box, but that is precisely
where John Wilkes Booth waits,
uncinched, holding what is
our future in his hand.

Fraidy-cat Kafka was terrified
of mice though he knew everything
could be pickled or toasted
or turned like boa constrictors
into belts.

I hope to grow old
kneading you. Failing that,
I jiffle like a hooked perch,
wanting to know not only
how you are but where.

Gymnopédie #1

Hear it? How the right hand insinuates,
hesitates, then encroaches again
on the resignation, his weariness
freed from all that Wagnerian sauerkraut
and bombast.
          Fired as second pianist
at Le Chat Noir, he played thousands
of requests at the Inn of the Nail
before he learned to respect the silence,
how much a meager melody can mean.

Hear it? How the paper between the strings
tamps the sound, compels the slow waltz
to submit.
         Satie's girlfriend, a trapeze
artist, ran off to the circus; she fed
her cats caviar while he ate white food—
sugar, minced bones, thirty-egg omelets—
and devoured oysters by the dozen. He wore
priestly robes though he lived in squalor.

Hear it? The idiosyncrasy: the shadow
of the lighthouse, the press of Spartan maidens
at dance, the minimalism of Man Ray
and Duchamp, all that pained sophistication
edging itself into the foreground.

Hear it? Furniture music destined to be
ignored, funeral tunes for an old century.

Popocatépetl and Iztaccihuatl

The chief's daughter, a beautiful princess,
fell in love with a handsome warrior
who, before heading into battle, asked
the old man for her hand. He left
with that promise in his heart.

Before long his rival Tlaxcala told the princess
that Popocatépetl had died in combat.
Like most lovers, she had expected disaster,
so she couldn't imagine what he said was a lie.

When Popocatépetl returned, he learned
of her death. Devastated, he wandered the streets
fearful his beloved might one day be forgotten.

He ordered a tomb—a pile of ten hills—
be brought together into a single mountain.
Then he carried her corpse to the summit
and committed her to everlasting sleep with a kiss.

Beneath the snow that covered them,
they became two volcanoes, the highest
in the hemisphere. The coward Tlaxcala
was overcome with repentance and went off
to die alone though he too became a mountain,

Pico de Orizaba, but one that was doomed forever
to see the two lovers who could not now be parted.
The Sleeping Woman's face is turned skyward.
Though she can't walk it, the path to her lover
is the route of conquistadors, Paso de Cortés.

Lead Belly's Undertaking

At the river I stand; guide my feet, hold my hand.

His suit fit him like a pigskin glove,
his Masonic apron in place
when they laid him behind the church
in Caddo Parish, a dozen miles
along the road to Mooringsport—

before Angola and the seven years
in Sugarland, before the women
and the fights. He was reared
the way he died, shoeless
on white man's soil.

Even his disease was named
for a white, though Gehrig
was made of stern stuff too.
Now both are as silent
as his Stella twelve-string.

Though music makes the eternal fleeting,
we shouldn't expect him back,
at least not soon or until we lead lives
worth singing about. Until then
he'll lie in Louisiana's fine, soft land.

The Terrorist

Bearded or not, his face mocks
the sick who struggle in the debris,
the frantic calamity of fire and flood
that merge like the call of bullfrogs and dark wings.

The human part almost disappears.
The girl gathering blossoms was never here,
though today other children stare at the sun
as if to read their futures in the hissing light.

But what remains has been feathered and cracked
by shards and space and cratered night.
What fell was cleft of mud,
a parliament of stones that once exploded
and scattered itself like bones,
leaving one life streaming toward the clouds
and another just like it tumbling back.

Misplaced Wishes

I always wanted to be somebody;
I guess I should have been more specific.

About the Author

Jerry Bradley, a member of the Texas Institute of Letters, is University Professor of English and the Leland Best Distinguished Faculty Fellow at Lamar University. He won the 2017 Boswell Poetry Prize awarded by Texas Christian University and in 2018 received writing awards from the Conference of College Teachers of English and the Texas College English Association. He is the author of 9 books including 4 other full-length poetry collections: *Simple Versions of Disaster* (University of North Texas Press), *The Importance of Elsewhere* (Ink Brush Press), *Crownfeathers and Effigies* (Lamar University Literary Press), and *South of the Boredom* (Angelina River Press).

Bradley's poems have appeared in *New England Review, American Literary Review, Modern Poetry Studies, Poetry Magazine*, and *Southern Humanities Review*. He is the long-time poetry editor of *Concho River Review*. He is also a past-president of the Texas Association of Creative Writing Teachers and the Southwest Popular and American Culture Association which endows a writing award in his name.

In 2014 Bradley was named a Piper Professor, an annual award that recognizes 10 top Texas professors. In 2000 he received the Joe D. Thomas Scholar-Teacher of the Year from the Texas College English Association and the 2005 Frances Hernandez Teacher-Scholar Award given by the Conference of College Teachers of English. He was named Outstanding Alumnus from Midwestern State University's College of Liberal Arts in 2002.

More information is available on his Wikipedia page (Jerry Bradley, poet) and personal website www.jerrybradley.net. He may be contacted at jerry.bradley@hotmail.com.